TOP 12

STOCK

TRADER

MISTAKES

and How to Avoid Them

Peter D Schneider

Copyright Information
C MMXIV Peter D. Schneider

All rights reserved.

Peter D. Schneider Bio

Peter D. (Pete) Schneider, founder of Discover Solutions Corp, is an accomplished business and investing entrepreneur, author, and success coach. His main website, howtotradeinthestockmarket .com, delivers the key ingredients for greater success in trading.

One of Pete's favorite quotes is by musician Charles Mingues: "Making the simple complicated is common place, making the complicated simple, awesomely simple, that's creativity."

Pete uses simple creativity with stories to accelerate the learning curve for beginning and intermediate independent traders. Even advanced traders have learned little gold nuggets of wisdom from Pete to improve their own trading results.

Having gained personal and financial freedom from selling his family business and then trading the stock market, his goal is to share, teach, train and coach clients to attain their own personal and financial freedom. Pete's inside knowledge of the stock market, along with easy-to-understand stories and illustrations provided to clients, helps them to be aware of what is happening in the stock markets today and, most importantly, to achieve more money-making trading successes and fewer money-losing stock trades.

Pete had the luxury of being trained by various successful traders and trading programs when he began his career in stock trading. Coming from an independent investor perspective and using a businessman's insights, he has learned the lessons of how and why the stock market works.

His e-books, webinars, training and personal coaching programs are all designed to answer the questions his clients have about trading the stock and options market successfully. Simply put, he makes the complicated easy to understand with insights, legal shortcuts and informative stories.

Pete's goal is to educate, equip and arm the independent trader to change the odds of winning in the favor of his clients, helping them to create financial independence.

SPECIAL INTRODUCTORY OFFER
Don't Get Left Behind!

Your **Personal Invitation from Peter Schneider**

Because you bought my book I'd like **personally INVITE YOU** to visit my blog and subscribe for updates so you can get the latest key insights into what's working in the world of stock trading, cool tools and new programs.

If you want to learn to make more money making trades and avoid making money-losing trades, then here's what I'd like to invite you to do.

Go ahead and log on to: www.howtotradeinthestockmarket.com and sign up for a free account. It takes less than 30 seconds and could very well revolutionize the way you think, take action and produce more winning trades.

That means you'll be able to get all the latest developments in stock trading, ALERTS, the reminders to pay attention to earnings calendars, coming earnings seasons and key upcoming critical market events.

You will also get alerts on my forthcoming book, "HOW TO TIME YOUR TRADE – for Greater Profits." As a special treat you will receive my first chapter in advance of the book's release in the middle of 2014.

Again, signing up is easy and FREE. Point your web browser to www.howtotradeinthestockmarket.com and sign up for free account (we promise to never spam or share your account information and name with anyone).

So if you have enjoyed this book and want to take your stock trading to the next level, head on over to www.howtotradeinthestockmarket.com right now and get on board for free.

What do you have to lose but your hard-earned money?

Table of Contents

Introduction

Welcome to "Top 12 Stock Trader Mistakes and How to avoid them." Right up front I want to tell you I've made all these mistakes to one degree or another.

As a matter of fact, because I entered stock and options trading full-time for myself in 1999 during the dot-com era, I experienced both the boom and then the bust. I made multi-millions and lost millions.

It's not like I pulled these mistakes out of thin air; I actually experienced the highs of trading successfully and then the pain and suffering of making these mistakes.

My purpose in writing this book is to give you, the independent trader, the information, tools and resources to become one of the 5 percent of long-term traders that become successful and not one of the 95 percent that wash out. I was lucky in 1999 to have sold our family business and have both wealth in time and money to get an education and go full-time into trading.

The sum total of the information in this book is what I would have wanted someone to read myself. I offer simple and insightful information that would put the odds of being successful on my side by placing money-making trades.

My goal is to provide you with simple-to-use information and stories to give you unique insights into the trading world. To empower you to become one of the 20 percent and create the degree of financial freedom you are seeking from additional income, supplemental retirement income or the 5 percent that achieve ultimate financial freedom.

As I see it, it is getting harder and harder to earn money by traditional methods as we get older. For those of you wishing to get involved or who are already involved with trading, this will help you become more successful, making money-making trades and avoid making money-losing trades.

The big boys and girls of Wall Street are here to make billions for their companies and clients while making millions in bonuses for themselves. They do not discriminate against anyone regardless of age, sex, race, religion, widows or orphans; they are here to win. In order to work in their world, we need to know how to avoid getting run over by their bus and how to navigate to produce money-making trades.

These mistakes are real. If you're making even one of them, it can cost you big time. But chances are, you're making multiples of these mistakes. It's time for us to get a handle on that and fix it.

Disclaimer

The purpose of this book is for general educational purposes only. The author is in no way acting as a financial adviser or investing broker and none of the ideas and concepts embodied in this book should be taken by the reader as recommendations to make specific investments.

The materials in this book are not a substitute for obtaining professional advice from a qualified person, firm or corporation. Consult the appropriate professional advisor for more current and complete information.

Top 12 Mistakes Stock Traders Make and Discover Solutions Corp is not engaged in rendering financial or legal services by placing these general materials in this book or website.

Top 12 Mistakes Stock Traders Make and Discover Solutions Corp specifically disclaims any liability, whether based in contract, tort, strict liability or otherwise, for any direct, indirect, incidental, consequential, or specific damages that arise out of or are in any way connected with the access to or use of Top 12 Mistakes Traders Make.

Top 12 Mistakes Traders Make and Discover Solutions Corp make no representations or warranties about the accuracy or completeness of the information contained in this book.

No part of this book may be reproduced or transmitted in any form by any means, graphic, electronic or mechanical, including photocopying, recording, taping by any means, or information storage or retrieval system, without the written permission of the author. The author and publisher of this book have made their best efforts in preparing this material for accuracy and completeness.

What We Will Cover

We're going to talk about the single biggest mistake people make with trading stocks. We'll discuss why this is critical for your stock trading, no matter what level of stock trader you are. We'll talk about what this means to your future, plus 12 specific stock-trading mistakes people make and how to fix them, and of course, much, much more.

The Biggest Stock-Trading Mistake

The biggest stock-trading mistake that I made and see people making all the time is not timing their trades. The fact is that building your trade around this one key piece of information dramatically changes your rate of success in stock trades. This is a game-changer. You need to accept this.

As I have said before, I didn't time my trades for the longest time. I didn't know and traded on charting information, a multitude of indicators and subscription recommendations.

I created too many losing trades and my trading account kept shrinking, growing smaller by trading. It wasn't until about four years ago when I stopped trading, reviewed my trades and found the missing key piece of information, then life changed.

Like any good trader, I went and did everything wrong, but didn't give up and broke through creating too many losing trades.

Why This Is Important

Why is timing your trades, and understanding these mistakes and how to fix them, so important? The statistics cited by leading experts really tells the whole story. The statistics on independent stock traders are that 95 percent will quit after losing their trading account starting equity.

The stated 95 percent is truth for the person who trades a few times with no education. Compiling studies indicates that 80 percent of traders produce negative trade results and 20 percent positive trades. Researchers attribute education and timing stock trades as the differentiator. Better trading skills increase success between 70 percent losers and 30 percent winners.

A number of studies and reports come to the same conclusion, that independent traders are cutting their winners early and letting their losing trades run. This is the exact opposite from the winning formula of cutting your losing trades early and letting your successful trades run.

There are millions of new individuals that are lured into the stock market yearly to seek some level of financial freedom. There are so many marketers screaming, "Make a fortune now!" Day traders have the quickest exit trading due to losses and exhausting their trading account.

Most traders jump into stocks that catch their eye due to sharp moves or media attention. I might add juicy emails and fancy mailbox brochures to that list.

Momentum traders jump in the biggest gainers and bargain hunters pile onto troubled issues.

In either case, they are dealing in a relatively small number of tradable stocks in the public arena and following a crowd is rarely a successful strategy unless you learn timing.

One study, "Quantitate Analysis of Investor Behavior," found that investors were so woefully inept at timing decisions that they managed to underperform the funds they were buying by a huge margin. This is just the tip of the iceberg.

Penalties for Not Preventing or Fixing These Mistakes

The penalties for doing this wrong, making these mistakes and ignoring this is you're missing out on making more money making stock trades. You are missing out on a ton of opportunities to make money and avoid losing trades.

If you have been around for a while, you're going to remember 2008, when the bull market crashed and wiped out billions of dollars and killed many investors' trading accounts, as well as their 401 and retirement accounts.

We have had a five-year run-up on this bull market. When we have a reversal in the stock market, the issue of timing a trade becomes even more critical to the independent stock trader to navigate to create money-making profitable trades. If you're not educated and well versed on how to time your trade, you are a sitting duck at the beginning of hunting season.

How This Is Different

Most books that talk about stock trading focus on strategies, indicators, methods and formulas. How to build a house, with what materials to use and how to put them together to make successful trades.

Still others share their key winning insights, magic formulas and never-before-revealed secrets to make quick, ungodly sums of money and retire rich beyond your wildest imagination.

This book is different. Some might say that talking about the mistakes is being negative. I disagree. When you know the pitfalls to avoid, and you learn to recognize the traps ahead of time, you can save yourself a TON of time, frustration AND money.

Plus, we humans learn by examples and stories. When we see what NOT to do, combined with solid advice on what to do instead, it creates a faster, more enduring learning experience. And, when it comes to something as important as your hard-earned money, you can't afford to take one second longer than necessary to start getting results.

Mistake #1

"Don't Use a Treasure Map to Find Trading Gold."

Mistake # 1 is that stock traders do not research their trades for the earnings release date and time.

Why is it a mistake?

Because without a written plan, most traders make up action plans that are subject to intuition, fear, paralysis and second-guessing.

This is a mistake because four times a year on a specific date and time, a trading wall is reached on every stock trade that after the release, an industry average of two out of three stocks price goes down. Most traders don't factor this event into their trade when they make it.

Every publically traded stock has to report to the Security and Exchange Commission (SEC) on a quarterly date, four times a year. The SEC requires audited financial results, among other requirements, and they have to be released to the stockholders of record and general public on a published specific day and time. The time is either before the market opens (BM) or after the market closes, (AM). No releases during an active day of trading.

Most active traders that I have met during numerous events, shows, and webinars do not know or have not factored in this critical information into their trading strategy or trading platform. Many private coaching clients had no idea how critical these dates and time are to their placing a successful trade.

What are the consequences of making this mistake and how critical are they?

Here are the consequences of not researching these earnings dates and times:

1. You are blind to the rules of the trading world and trade at a huge disadvantage, making many trades at exactly the wrong time and creating money-losing trades.
2. You make a trade at the right time and start making money, but all of a sudden your stock goes down and you lose money because your trade went over this earnings date and time, creating a losing trade.
3. You have a winning trade and add to your position, and after a period of time your stock goes down for no apparent reason; your trade passed over its earning release date and time, and you are left with a money-losing trade.
4. You make a trade at the right time and it goes higher, and one day it jumps even higher and you don't know why (after an earnings release date and time), as it continues to grow as a winning trade. The results is you think you think have the

magic formula, strategy, trading platform or advisor service that is bulletproof.

Why traders tend to make these mistakes.

Traders make these mistakes for two reasons: education and automation.

Education

A. No one has taught them about the critical importance of earnings release and time so they just are not aware of the fundamental ground rules of trading.
B. Traders get caught up in all the indicators and tools they use to analyze their trades and do not factor in this basic quarterly time frame.
C. Traders rely on a stock-picking service or subscription to tell them about the trade and these never mention earnings date dangers.

Automation

Traders buy a fully automated trading platform that does not include any mention of impending quarterly earnings release dates and time. They simply use a buy signal, green light or combination of indicators to enter a trade and an exit signal, a red light, to exit a position.

I learned from a few private coaching clients that had been using these programs that the entry or exit signals do not factor in the earnings date and time into the system and/or platform.

Many times the exit signal was given after the earnings date and time had already had been released and the exit signal was a lagging indicator which already created a money-losing trade. This discovery was unearthed with a post-mortem review, which I call a stock trade autopsy. It's amazing what you find out if you're willing to examine your losing trades.

Insight story

My personal story was that even as a well-educated trader with all the expensive stock trading training, live events, CDs, DVDs, books and trading platforms, I still created too many money losing trades.

I kept thinking about WHY my trades were going bad, and when the market went from bullish to bearish in 2000, I had long strings of more money-losing trades.

Until I learned what happens before, during and after a company's earnings release day and time, a high percentage of my trades lost serious money. The pattern repeated itself until I researched and learned the basic secrets to trading earnings releases successfully.

Every fellow trader I have talked to has been burned and has taken big losses from not knowing what happens during earnings release periods and how to actually trade those events. Once I learned the lessons, my stock trading became much more successful and consistent.

What should you do if you have already made this mistake? How do you fix it?

If you are in a trade:

    A. Immediately go and research your active trade to the next earnings date and time.

    B. Free – go to yahoofinance.com and type in your ticker symbol and look for earnings release. Get confirmed date and time of next quarter's release information.

    C. See where you are in your trade – early, during, right on or after the release date – and see how your stock trade is performing.

Expert advice

The majority of experts in the trading community advise that you should not hold over short-term trades of a company's release. This is a whole class in trading that you should take, that I will be teaching in the future.

How do we avoid making this mistake moving forward.

    1. Pick the stock you want to trade and first research these two pieces of key information: earnings release date and time.

    2. Free – go to yahoofinance.com and type in your ticker symbol and look for earnings release. Get

confirmed date and time of next quarter's release information.

3. Have a print calendar preferably a one-page yearly calendar at your desk.

   Circle that date and time of the trade you've researched. Look at the date and time of the day you do this and look where you are relative to that date. Trade accordingly to that time frame. Hint, you can set your smart phone to alert you to this time deadline that is looming.

Here is how you can get results faster, easier, and more efficiently

Here's how you should avoid making this mistake moving forward...

A. Research every trade with the next earnings date and time.

B. Place your trade after earnings season is over and settled down by two weeks.

C. Each earnings season is approximately 90 days apart; use your trading tools and plan/strategy to plan your trade. Get educated on how to time your trade for great success and profitability.

The two best tools for researching your next trade are:

1. http://biz.yahoo.com/research/earncal/today.html

2.http://www.nasdaq.com/earnings/earnings-calendar.aspx

The big insight

Here is my biggest, most insightful advice to you for your trading success.

Find the next earnings date and time for your next potential trade. It doesn't matter whether you found the trade, it was a hot tip from any source, or came from your financial advisor, stock broker or stock selection service – research it.

Check any trades against that date and follow how that trade did as it approached the earnings date and time and as the event happened.

A vast majority of experts advise that a short-term trader should exit a trade before the earnings release because about two out of three trades stalls and go down after the company's earnings release.

Long-term traders should be watching earnings release and time to determine if it's time to exit that trade because the trade is not performing per your long-term written trading plan.

There is a whole course you should take around how to time your trade. Reference

howtotimeyourstocktrade:
www.howtotradeinthestockmarket.com .

Yes, this is a course I offer because its information I have never learned from anyone in all the years I have traded. This information is extremely powerful and changes the odds of you making more money-making trades and avoiding money-losing trades.

Summary

Let's summarize:

1. If you don't use earnings release and time, you are trading blind.
2. You need this information (earnings release and time) on every trade to time your trade between earnings seasons.
3. You dramatically increase your odds by researching and using earnings release and time to make winning trades and equally avoid money-losing trades. This will help you become a smarter, more successful trader.

Now that we have conquered timing the market with Mistake #1, it's time to go over how to avoid Mistake #2 – not factoring in critical timing events.

Mistake #2
"Why Men Don't Ask for Directions."

Mistake # 2 is that traders don't factor in the CRITICAL yearly calendar of earnings seasons, Federal Reserve meetings, stock options expiration dates and surprise events.

Why is this a mistake?

This is a mistake because every one of these timeframes and actual dates affect the overall environment in setting up a winning stock trade. Overlook any of these dates and you may be setting yourself up to time your entry point of your trade incorrectly and set up a losing trade.

The consequences of this mistake are critical when it comes to the percentage of winning trades you place versus the money-losing trades you make.

What are the consequences of making this mistake and how critical are they?

1. You are trading blind.
2. You do not have a concrete foundation in place to make winning trades.
3. The events of the season and dates disrupt your trading plan, even if it's for a day or more, which leads to your confusion and frustration as a confident trader.

Why and when do traders tend to make this mistake?

Traders make this mistake because:

A. You have not been taught the significance of these seasons and dates.
B. You do not factor them into your trading plan.
C. You do not have any source that warns you of these impending seasons and dates.
D. You do not have a one-page printed calendar on your trading desk to refer to.

Insight story, from a private client of mine:

Mary (named changed) bought an automated trading package after attending a free national tour of speakers in her area.

I knew Mary as a member of a coaching mastermind group that I belonged to as a business coach. She knew I was a successful active individual trader and wanted to get some pointers after making this purchase. She was excited and shared with me her desire to make a substantial income for her $3,000 annual subscription fee to this service.

I reviewed her program and her 10 beginning trades, most of which had gone bad. As we dissected her trades, I asked her a number of questions and it quickly became apparent that there was missing timing information in her system. The system was buy on a green signal and then sell on a red signal.

From my training, and most importantly, my failed trades, I uncovered why Mary was having so many money-losing trades. The system and Mary never factored in the CRITICAL calendar events that take place.

Once we built a trading plan around the system she bought, we increased her success rate to the point of Mary being able to go to the BMW local dealership and pay cash for a brand new 328I convertible. Talk about living the good life, driving around Tucson, AZ, with a smile on her face, enjoying her success.

What you should do instead

What traders like you should do if you're making these mistakes:

Two-part Strategy: Master Calendar and Critical Dates

A. Master Calendar

1. Get a one-page yearly calendar. Print it out.
2. Earnings Calendar – Underline continuous line with a RED pen – January, February, March; then April, May, June; next, July, August, September; and lastly, October, November, December. These are the calendar earnings seasons.
3. Earnings Release months (majority) – Get a green pen and circle January, April, July, October.

B. Critical Dates

1. Google the next Federal Reserve meeting dates and enter them in your Calendar.

2. From Mistake #1 – research your next earnings release dates and times and enter them on your calendar or trading tracker written document.

3. First thing, scan your Internet search engine for news that is unexpected: think 9-11, tsunamis, hurricanes, and wars. Anything that is unexpected from the stock market perspective has to be factored in to determine if it's good or bad news and may take instant direction on the market and or your trade, or a day or two while the market digests.

Take this Master Calendar and see where you are relative to your trade. If in doubt, set your stops and or exit a position based on your trading plan or platform.

How to prevent making this mistake moving forward...

Use the two sets of action items from above (MASTER CALENDAR and CRITICAL DATES) and prepare your Master Trading Calendar and use it to time your future trades.

FREE – Cool tool to help you make more successful trades and avoid making money losing trades. Go to www.howtotradeinthestockmarket.com/cooltool/Master Calendar

The KEY – Plan your trade and trade your plan. By building these key pieces of information into your written trading plan you are building a foundation for successful trading, moving the odds in your favor to enter money-making trades and avoiding money-losing trades.

Let's summarize:

A. Traders don't factor in critical yearly calendar events.

B. Traders are blind to ongoing events that effect the market and their trades.

C. With one Cool Tool you dramatically change the odds of making more money-making trades and avoiding money-losing trades.

Now that we've gotten past Mistake #2, critical calendar mistakes, it's time to go over how to avoid Mistake #3, written plan.

"Why You Shouldn't Drive Drunk at Night with Your Headlights Off."

Mistake #3 is that traders do not have a written trading plan in place.

Why is it a mistake?

1. Because without a written plan most traders make up action plans on the fly that are subject to intuition, fear, inaction and second-guessing.
2. In emergency situations, you do not have an action plan to refer to on the steps to deal with a positive response.
3. Because all long-term successful independent traders have told me they have written trading plans or automated trading systems based on written rules.

What are the consequences of making this mistake and how critical are they?

A. In a critical moment, people—and traders more so—tend to freeze in decision-making, resulting in bigger money-losing trades.

B. Stock trading calls for decisions to be made before you even make your trade or all you will do is make money-losing trades.

C. If all long-term successful independent traders have a written plan, how do you think you're going to become successful long-term without one?

Why and when do traders tend to make this mistake?

1. Traders make this mistake because no one has taught them to write a simple written trading plan.
2. If they do have a written plan, traders tend not to modify them with the trading experiences they learn, new tools they use or new education they have taken.
3. In the heat of the trade, which calls for an immediate decision, traders just grab their emergency written plan and act on it.

Insight story

My story starts with selling our family business in 1999 and leaving my CEO position and signing a non-compete agreement. I had no place to go, with money and time, so with the help of a friend, got into the stock and options trading world.

I learned a lot and made millions and lost millions in the Internet bubble and bust. I learned great ways to make money and horrible ways to lose money. Every lesson was a piece of my trading plan.

For the longest time I just flew by the seat of my pants in my trading activities. I never became successful over the long run until I developed my own SIMPLE written trading plan. Because the stock market is a living thing I have found that my trading plan has to be viewed as a living document.

This means from time to time I need to review my plan and adjust it; this mostly happens when I have too many money-losing trades in a row. Yes, I do have money-losing trades, because its part of the way the market works in its mystery as it lives. You have to incorporate that into your written plan as well.

What should they do instead.

A. Learn to write a simple stock trading plan.
B. Write down the steps you are already doing in finding a stock, researching a stock, placing the order, and target profit and exit points based on a successful or failing trade.
C. Focus on your exit strategy and automate it by using tools like trailing stops because exiting a trade is the hardest part of trading.

What should you do if you have already made this mistake? How do you fix it?

1. If you have an active trade or trades going, write out the exit choices you have in front of you. Write them down, even if it's on the back of a napkin. Act on the best choice.

2. STOP TRADING if your trades are losing money. If you don't have a written plan, get one, make one and/or learn to make one.
3. If you have winning and losing trades, write out the actions you took to produce winning trades in your written trading plan.

How do we prevent making this mistake moving forward?

1. Make a written simple trading plan based on what you learned and what is working for you.
2. If you have bought a trading platform, trading courses and trading tools, distill them down into a written trading plan.
3. Research trading plans on Google and print out a few and use them as your template on the trading steps you are taking.

Here is how you can get results faster, easier, and more efficiently:

Start your written plan by using my FREE Earnings Calendar.

www.Howtotradeinthestockmarket.com/cooltool/tradingcalendar

Let's summarize:

1. No written trading plan to work with leads to many money-losing trades.
2. Traders tend to freeze when confronted with unplanned events and market changes.

3. All long-term active independent traders have a written trading plan or system that has been based on written action steps.

Now that we know having a written trading action plan can wipe out a major mistake stock traders make, we can tackle Mistake #4.

Mistake #4

"The Magic Button."

Mistake # 4 is trading is an easy way to get rich.

Why is this a mistake?

This is a mistake because stock trading is not making the big money-making trades easily, quickly, in little time, despite what is sold and promoted to the unsuspecting public.

Trading is like gambling in Las Vegas, where the odds are stacked against you; there are bigger, more powerful players you are betting against; and there are rules, strategies and systems that the big boys and girls who work for the top Wall Street firms use that you don't know about.

This is also a mistake because stock trading is like the game of baseball, where a player hits successfully 2.50 times out of 10 times up. That is the average that is estimated by industry experts that beginning to intermediate traders reach as a success rate.

The trading game is about getting base hits: singles, doubles but not grand slams. No one tells new traders that this is the benchmark and mindset to start your trading experience from.

What are the consequences of making this mistake and how critical are they? There are two parts to this section: Gambling and Shame

Gambling

1. Traders have the mindset that this is like buying a winning lottery ticket, where all you have to do is buy a ticket, sit back and collect on your purchase.
2. Traders are not prepared to get themselves educated, practice trading plans and treat trading as a business, not going to Vegas to gamble.
3. Get excited, focus your attention and money-making opportunities, unprepared to lose it all.

Shame

A. Lose your money quickly, get frustrated and quit.
B. Quit because you have no additional money to invest in education and further trading.
C. Have a lifelong story of how you got screwed and taken advantage of by the thieves from Wall Street.

Insight story

In April of 1999 my friend and I went into stock trading full-time after our company got bought up and we received an employment buyout package. My friend Ed bought a $6,000 package which was for two people so I bought my half from him. We had purchased a great trading package with systems, education and cool tools.

Luckily we had time and money to trade. As luck would have it, we were at the dot-com boom and the stock market went to new all-time highs. Our trading accounts went up quickly, crazy with a majority of wins.

Almost a year later came the dot-com bomb and everything went to crap real quickly. We had many losses and had to go back to basics to learn to really trade to be successful. Part of trading success is timing the market and timing the company's performance.

What we had to do is learn basics, have sound strategies and tie them into written trading plans. We were lucky to hit the market right but it turned out we had to do the homework to make long-term success in all phases of ups and downs in the market.

What should they do instead?

Plan this as starting your own little business that you can grow. Industry statistics estimate that the average starting account for beginning traders is $1,500 to $5,000 dollars in size.

Two parts: Basics and Ongoing

A. Basics
1. Learn how the stock market works from a few beginners books and references
2. When you research stock trading companies who you want to open an account with, research their free trainings. There are a lot of great free trading resources.

3. Develop a written trading plan and use that as your guide.

B. Ongoing

1. Research and buy a trading platform or trading program that teaches you about trading.
2. Learn how to cut your loses quickly with trading stops and let your winners run with trailing stops. These features will be offered and you can learn about them free from a reputable trading company that you set up your trading account with.
3. **Use** the information in the book to time your trades and sign up at www.howtotimeyourtrade.com for free e-mails and updates to grow your trading successes.

What should you do if you have already made this mistake? How do you fix it?

1. Stop trading and get educated.
2. Develop and implement a trading plan for you to follow.
3. Mindset is everything: move from gunslinger or flying by the seat of your pants to working your successful trades.

How do we prevent making this mistake moving forward?

Two Parts: Don'ts and Do's

A. Don'ts

1. Do not think that making money from stock trading is like buying a lottery ticket and winning the top prize or someone selling you how to pick and buy that grand slam stock trade.
2. Do not sign up for too many free e-mails or newsletters that get can you overwhelmed with information.
3. Do not buy a course that sounds too good to be true because there is some work involved in becoming a successful trader.

B. Do's

1. Take some courses from seasoned industry professionals who admit they have lost money before they learned how to make money by learning the insights, rules and strategies on how to work the stock market, not play the stock market.
2. This means reading, taking webinars and watching videos, which are so abundant and free that the only real investment is your time and dedication.
3. Consider buying a trading system that is reputable for you to launch your trading from. Be sure to research comments on Google.com to verify the credibility of the system you are thinking of buying.

Here is how you can get results faster, easier, and more efficiently:

Take the lessons in this book and get your free cool tool to set up your trading calendar today.

www.howtotradeinthestockmarket/cooltool/mastercalendar.

The key. Learn how the market works, why it reacts the way it does, and how to stay small and nimble in a big, fast-paced world. Don't step in front of a big, fast-moving Wall Street bus.

Summary

1. Trading is not an easy way to get instantly rich.
2. Education is the key to learning how to go from playing the market (gambling) to working the market for learning to time successful trades.
3. Cutting off your losing trades quickly and letting your winning trades run is how you go from the average 2.5 winning trades per 10 to 3–5 winning trades per 10 or better depending on your systems and rules you follow.

Now that we have covered Mistake #4, Getting Rich, we will move to Mistake #5, Analysis Paralysis.

Mistake #5

"I Love to Make Things Difficult."

Mistake #5 is having analysis paralysis.

Why is it a mistake?

There are simply too many sources of information, available tools, strategies to use and conflicting rules to creating a successful trade. Traders buy way too many products and services without enough time to learn the details to build a successful written successful trading plan.

What are the consequences of making this mistake and how critical are they? Consequences are two parts: Frozen and Searching

Frozen

1. Traders can't make a timely decision to enter or exit a trade.
2. Traders feel doubt about what to do next.
3. Traders get FROZEN in their trading plan, endless researching, looking at indicators, studying what they have bought in books, training and subscriptions.

Searching

1. Look at the inbox of e-mails; notice the flood of them with the newest, make-money strategies.
2. Get stock traders' overwhelm.
3. Work on everything else but trading stock. Complete mindless and useless little projects.

Why and when do traders tend to make this mistake?

Two parts: New Tools and Paralysis

New tools

1. When a trader looks for a silver bullet to build their trading success on.
2. When a trader looks for every new, glittery, well-written marketing e-mail or brochure that comes their way to gain successful trading.
3. When the trader produces too many money-losing trades.

Paralysis

1. When traders don't believe they have the insights and instincts to build their trading platform.
2. When a trading system or advice from an expert leaves them with too many losing stock trades and not enough trading funds.
4. Traders second-guess themselves at every step of the trading written action plan they have for

themselves. This is most evident when traders are trading by the seat of their pants.

Insight story

One of my private clients, Greg, is an airline pilot. He is a captain at a major airline. He was making too many losing trades when his wife's friend, Alice, recommended he give me a call. It seems Greg had taken many courses and read many books in his 10-year trading career. His analytical mind went crazy with all the indicators, strategies and decisions he was faced with in his daily trading life. Many times he was in the air and away from his computer and when he landed, half the time he was in different time zones and countries.

After he contacted me and we had our first getting-to-know-each other call, I could tell that Greg had analysis paralysis when it came to stock trading. We set up a private coaching program and we went to work on separating out what he needed to focus on and what he needed to put in the background. After a number of sessions it dawned on Greg that he had the answer to his situation. He made the following observations.

He sees stock trading as having the three things he needs as a pilot to have a successful flight.

A.   A preflight written checklist; has what he needs to check basics and key indicators.
B.   A monitoring checklist as his flight progresses.
C.   Final checklist after flight is completed.

My advice to him was to make it complete, timely and effective so that you can take off, fly and land in a prescribed amount of time. We worked on designing such a plan for him to trade on and it's getting wonderful results.

Greg is feeling great and confident in his trading and results and no longer feels the frustrations, sleepless nights and fear.

What should they do instead?

A. SIMPLIFY YOUR TRADING.
B. Get a yearly printed-out calendar and enter earnings seasons, earnings release months. Get it from my website,
www.howtotradeinthestockmarket.com/cooltool/tradingcalendar
C. Use the 80/20 rule: 80 percent of your success comes from 20 percent of the information that you process. Build a sound, easy-to-use written trading plan.

What should you do if you have already made this mistake? How do you fix it?

1. You should have a written trading plan, or if you're like most traders who don't have a trading plan and are flying by the seat of their pants, write out the steps you go through researching your trade.
2. Scratch off 80 percent of the steps of the steps you have set in your trading strategy, regardless if it's a written or on-the-fly trading plan. Turn 10 steps or 20 steps in your plan into half that.

3. Now add back a few that actually have value, no more than 2 to 4 steps to equal 8 or 16 steps.
4. Paper-trade your simplified trade plan.
5. Modify, plan and research until you get a working model to easily and quickly trade by.

How do we prevent making this mistake moving forward?

A. Always have the word SIMPLIFY in the forefront of your trading mind.
B. Develop a written trading plan that uses the most effective, least amount of time and tools to get you the answers you need to make a decision to trade or not trade that company you researched.
C. Buy one service that provides training, tools and a trading platform that simplifies all the data sources you use.

Here is how you can get results faster, easier, and more efficiently:

I'm a visual person so if I can't see what is going on for myself, I can't get my trading mind around what is going on. I like free tools and websites, but they only get you so far.

You have to know yourself where you can get what you're trying to achieve with the right tools and research. I found simpler is better.

My one great leverage: The key to my own success is Worden.com (My link) charting service. You can get a free 30-day trial and beyond that a very reasonable monthly subscription service, and discounts for a yearly rate. It is a powerful tool for researching and placing trades.

If you want to learn how I use my Worden charting service, go to

howtotimeyourtrade.com/worden3keycharts

Let's summarize:

1. Trading information, choice and speed is overwhelming, like the first time you go gambling in Vegas.
2. There is no silver bullet to trading, just basic homework.
3. Simple is better.
4. There are tools to simplify your trade; find them and use them.

Now that we have tamed Mistake #5, Analysis Paralysis, we can tackle Mistake #6, Relying on Experts.

Mistake #6

"It's all about the Benjamin's."

Mistake #6 is that traders don't follow the money.

Why is it a mistake?

When traders don't follow the money, it moves so fast that the trade hangs out to dry and turns into a money-losing trade.

When and why do traders make this mistake?

Many traders don't get educated in the fundamentals of money movement.

Money goes to where it is most appreciated and where it can appreciate the most. One symbol for the stock market is the bull. The smartest, fittest leaders of the bulls go to where the grass is the richest, greenest and most abundantly growing.

In the movie *All the President's Men*, the famous quote by Deep Throat was, **"Follow the Money."** Deep Throat, the government insider, pointed the two news reporters Bernstein and Woodward to find who was at the top of the Watergate scandal. "Follow the money" led them ultimately to the president of the United States.

Wall Street is no different. Find out who controls the money; that's where the bulls are. The term used most often is Smart Money for these leaders who make markets and stocks react one way or another, either going up or down in price.

What are the consequences of making this trading mistake and how critical are they?

Two parts: Disadvantage and Lost Opportunity

Disadvantage

1. You are at a huge disadvantage when a stock reverses course and the money stream goes down. This means the bulls are leaving for other, greener fields.
2. You are placing trades at the wrong time, creating money-losing trades.
3. You can hold onto a stock whose money stream is really tanking and getting worse.

Lost opportunity

1. When the money first starts flowing into the stock, you don't know it.
2. When the money flow surges in, you don't know it or see it.
3. When the money stream is going parabolic (straight up) like a rocket.

Why and when do traders tend to make this mistake?

When they have never been educated about this indicator being available to research a trade. If you don't know if the money stream is flowing into a stock, going sideways or leaving the stock, you are at a disadvantage.

You can use a variety of indicators and combinations to focus your trading plan for success but unless you follow the money, they don't tell the whole story.

Most of the money flow indicators are proprietary and you will have to buy the service to get the information. What you don't know will hurt you.

Insight story

Six months ago, I was working with my mentor/Internet marketing coach and found out Jim was interested in a few select stocks that he had traded and was considering for future trades. I shared with Jim the insights and tools I use to pick, research and evaluate potential stock trades.

I found out that by chance he was also a subscriber to Worden.com and we opened up our programs. I showed him the money tool and we proceeded to research Netflix and Facebook. As we dove into the charts, everything became crystal clear to what he was thinking and evaluating about the stocks and others too.

As we went back in time, Jim saw when he was following Netflix how it dove down after a business decision to raise rates, which he felt was a stupid move that would crash the stock price. Low and behold, it was and the money stream was confirming that fact.

Later, when Netflix made another bold move with Disney, the stock he felt was poised to go parabolic (through the roof) and it did. Jim was amazed with the cool tool and we researched other trades and fantastic research and confirmations appeared out of thin air.

Jim said it was one of the" best tools" he had ever seen.

What should they do instead?

A. Watch the movie *Jerry Maguire*; the title character is played by Tom Cruise, who asked, **"SHOW ME THE MONEY."** It's all about the money, who controls it, and leadership and how and when it's used in the stock trading world.

B. Get a free 30-day subscription from Worden**.com and get familiar with the proprietary money stream.**

C. Consider buying Worden's training video library program because this gives the very best, high-quality training and insights on how to use this indicator and other highly valuable tools.

What should you do if you have already made this mistake? How do you fix it? Two parts: Action and Research Your Trade.

Action

1. Get a free 30-day subscription from Worden.com

2. Get familiar with the proprietary money stream. Find out about tutorials for money stream. Worden tutorial video library.

Research your trade

1. After purchasing a free 30-day trial, create a three-chart page, showing Candlesticks, next chart Money Flow, and last, Daily Volume. Get a visual of what your open stock trade is doing.
2. Look at the stock trade you want to make next and visually see if the money is going in, hesitating or leaving your stock trade. If the money is leaving your stock trade, look to exit it as quickly as you deem appropriate.
3. Adjust your written trading plan to reflect this new and powerful tool.

How do we prevent making this mistake moving forward?

Incorporate at a minimum Money Stream from Worden.com to get a visual on following the money in any trade you are evaluating to make. The full charting service from Worden is robust and very reasonably priced. It is a tool you should be using.

The KEY here is how you can get results faster, easier, and more efficiently.

1. Get the Worden.com program and research your potential stock trade.
2. Use your written stock trading plan to enter and exit your stock trade.

3. Monitor your active stock trade by reviewing the money flow daily.

Buy a subscription to Wordentrainingvideolibrary.com for only $249.99 and get training on how to use money stream, selecting stocks and a number of other great videos.

Summary

1. If you don't know how to follow the money stream in your trade, you are trading by the seat of your pants and are at distinct disadvantage.
2. Money goes where it most is appreciated and can appreciate most.
3. Buy this powerful tool because it can make you more money-making trades and help you avoid making money-losing trades.

Now that we have overcome the mistake of not trading blind by being able to "Follow the Money," we will move onto Mistake #7.

Mistake #7

"Digging Your Own Grave."

Mistake #7 is to assume your education, work experience and life lessons translate into stock trading expertise.

Why is it a mistake?

If you're not educated in trading, have trader-related work experience and had a trader's life, the transfer of combined expertise is dangerous.

There may be some advantages but they are outweighed by assumptions, insights, shortcuts and rules for success that you learned that simply don't apply to the world of trading.

What are the consequences of making this mistake and how critical are they?

1. Your logic, line of thinking, reasoning and conclusions of how the stock market works is flawed and filtered to what you know to be true from a culmination of life experiences. This thought process puts you at a disadvantage and can cause trades to be made at wrong times, valuations and sets you up for money-losing trades.

2. How you solved problems, anticipated coming events and prepared for potential emergencies did not prepare you for how the stock market reacts and how quickly it can shift gears going up, down or sideways. You are truly unprepared for market trading rules and will be blindsided in your trading abilities.

3. Traders think they know the market and read the charts but many traders don't know that a huge percentage of trades are done on computers that have been pre-programmed to trade when certain criteria are met or realized. You don't stand a chance of long-term success unless you know how and why the market does what it does.

Why and when do traders tend to make these mistakes?

There are many times this can happen, with three major times coming to mind.

1. When the person first decides to become a trader they just make the assumption that this will be easy to master because they have achieved great success in their lives and/or work environment. They buy some training program and immediately start to trade and get tumbled with their trades and lose money.

2. The person buys a trading platform and relies on a signal to get in and then exit a trade. The trading package has training modules, some good and some even excellent. The trader skims the information and starts trading and gets mixed,

frustrating results. Makes too many money-losing trades.

3. The trade goes through some good trading training and start to achieve some success in a good bull market (up-trending) and comes into market that switches to a bear (down-trending) pattern. Uses information that worked in bull markets but not bear markets and gets too many money-losing trades.

What should they do instead?

A. Become a freshman student and take training and webinars that teach you stock trading basics. If you set up an account with a reputable stock brokerage firm, they should have great tutorials.

B. Education is a key part of becoming a seasoned, experienced trader that survives for the long run. Read a few bestselling books. A few key books are listed in the back of this book.

C. Seek out seasoned, experienced teachers, trainers and coaches to read, train and learn from. The difference between an expert and EX PURT is that the expert will tell you they had to lose money and learn to become a good successful trader, where the EX PURT will simply tell you they are "great" and they know the way to a great shortcut, leading-edge insight and magic formula. See Mistake #8 for further definition.

What should you do if you have already made this mistake? How do you fix it?

1. STOP TRADING if your trading plan is not working.
2. Exit trades per your written trading plan, close trades and STOP TRADING.
3. Get a basic education from a book (recommendations in back of this book), training program from a stock trading broker, and/or a basic stock trading platform.

How do we prevent making this mistake moving forward?

A. Start as a student, fresh, with no preconceived ideas.
B. Read, listen and watch real professionals give their tips, insights and trading tools to go to battle with the stock market professionals. Write these down in a master trading file.
C. Learn to become a stock trader that thinks, reacts and feels like the market does in seasoning wisdom and insight to how the market REALLY works.

Insight story

I met Bruce at a traders' training program in Salt Lake City in 2008. He was a retired engineering department manager from a Fortune 500 company he had worked for 25 years.

We became friends and started talking trades, strategies and results. After some trust-building we started to talk about how well we did with what we knew and learned lessons from our business experiences.

As we talked, Bruce's trading assumptions became apparent and they reflected in his trading success and failures. As we discussed the painful lessons I had learned when I assumed how the market worked, Bruce realized he was making the same mistakes.

Some mistakes Bruce made no sense until he shared what he assumed he knew about the market. Until we discussed that the market does not always follow reason but acts on emotions and herd mentality, Bruce found that all he had learned did not transfer to his trading strategies and success.

Bruce had shared that his wife was a very emotional lady and I asked him this simple question: Do your work experience, strategies and management tools work on her for consistent results? Bruce said, "Hell, no." I then said, "Well, you have to adjust everything you know, see and feel because the stock market is like an emotional person."

It's never the same from day to day and you need to understand that and develop trading skills to become successful at trading. Bruce and I are still friends and we laugh when the market has a tizzy fit and we need to learn to deal with it.

Here is how you can get results faster, easier, and more efficiently:

1. Buy and read these two books from Amazon

A. The Warren Buffett Way by Robert G. Hagstrom

B. Trading for a Living by Alexander Elder

2. Invest an initial 10 hours of time to take the tutorials from your reputable stock trading company and/or stock trading training course or webinar.

3. Develop a written trading plan based on basic trading rules.

The key insight: My advice is, most parents if they can afford it send their graduating high school teenager to a college or university. The idea is to get their child a good education to be able to make a bigger income so they can live a better life. You should be using the same reasoning for yourself in investing in your education and trading tools, if you plan to derive a substantial income from stock trading for additional income, replacement income from retirement and/or ultimate financial freedom.

Summary

1. Assuming your life experiences will guide your trading success is wrong.
2. Traders need to prepare for their new profession at whatever level they choose to operate at.
3. Long-term successful trading depends on getting educated as a trader with a trader's skills and mindset.

Transitioning from this mistake, "Assuming your skills will transfer to success," we will tackle Mistake #8, Listening to Experts.

Mistake #8

"I Want to Hang Out with Rock Stars."

Mistake #8 is to listen and take everything from experts at full face value.

Why is it a mistake?

Stock trading experts are motivated to give you their view of how, when and why to trade stocks which can be detrimental to welfare of the independent stock trader. Numerous experts are geared to make money for their company and themselves and are not there for your best interests.

When the stock markets of the world trade in the trillions of dollars and billions of dollars are paid out in bonuses, it lends itself to produce experts everywhere you look.

Stock traders tend to look for expert leadership and guidance and choose someone that they can identify with. Many beginning stock traders look to TV shows to guide them and identify with the anchors, show hosts or guest experts.

Experts grow like weeds that are so prolific that they produce information overload, conflicting advice, strategies and rules to follow.

The stock market value is estimated by Wikipedia to be, worldwide, $36.6 trillion. U.S. markets are estimated at $16.6 trillion, with $267 billion in bonuses paid out in the U.S. in 2013.

What are the consequences of making this mistake and how critical are they?

1. If traders don't first research the experts you are exposed to and determine if they are in your best interests to listen to, you will produce money-losing trades.
2. If traders don't first research their trades, strategies or trading tools, per your written trading plan and your trading tools, you will produce many money-losing trades.
3. If traders believe the wrong experts, that belief of what is happening in the stock market will be warped and you will make all the wrong assumptions that lead to most independent stock traders losing all their money in their first year of trading.

Why and when do traders make this mistake?

A. New traders tend to make this mistake when they tune into TV programs that are focused on the stock market, active streaming quotes, that have anchors and guest experts commenting on what's happening in the stock market.
B. When traders hear and see a new pitch from a newsletter, e-mail and or mailed advertisement.

C. When traders hear and see a celebrity in the stock trading world and get the "I want to be a famous rock star, idea and hang out with rock stars syndrome.

What should they do instead?

1. Seek out true experts that are seasoned professionals with great reputations. One person who comes to mind is Warren Buffett, who has written great books, is very successful and has a sterling reputation.

2. Research the Internet when you find an expert and see what it has to say on that person. If they have written a book, go to Amazon and read the reviews.

3. Find other traders, stock advisors, and stock brokerage companies that have had success, and get recommendations and do your research.

What should you do if you have already made this mistake? How do you fix it?

A. When watching live TV trading programs, mute the program and just watch the streaming quotes.

B. Make a list of who you are looking at as experts and research their recommendations with the tools you have learned in this book. If their advice and trades make you money, keep them. If they add to your money-losing trades and cause confusion to your written trading plan, dump them and delete their e-mails and advertising.

C. Clean up your incoming e-mails from all core experts and advice you use. The continuous Internet marketing e-mails are all distracting and add to confusion.

How do we prevent making this mistake moving forward?

1. Researching your expert will separate the knowledgeable successful seasoned professional from the EX PURT. Definition is EX= has been, and Purt is a water drip under pressure, for a little trading humor. Make a list of your experts you follow.
2. Get a subscription after researching the possibilities on market commentary, stock selection and/or education that you can build your written stock trading plan on.
3. Do not listen to any other experts, marketing efforts, or shiny new tools that you do not research first. Focus your time and efforts to creating successful money-making trades and avoiding money-losing trades.

Here is how you can get results faster, easier, and more efficiently:

A. Look to a person or business that has had long-term success; focus on the individual stock trader's/investor's long-term success.
B. **Their success is a result of your success**.
C. Reviews of their companies and/or themselves are first-rate and the followers are loyalists.

The key:

Invest in advice from a respected, seasoned, successful professional.

Three that come to mind:

DISCLAIMER AS THE AUTHOR – I use these three.

1. Warren Buffet – *The Intelligent Investor* and other books.
2. Worden.com – This is a multi-generational family business focused on the individual trader. They are a charting service and help find trades based on formulas they write or you can write/modify. They provide Worden notes for Market Commentary and insights..
3. The Motley Fool - two brothers, David and Tom Gardner, have created this publication/subscription service for selecting stocks, market commentary and trader fellowship.

All three have built their success on first building their readers/subscribers or investors' success.

Summary

A. Stock trading is a multitrillion-dollar market making multibillion-dollar bonuses, creating opportunities for experts to sell everything related to stock trading, not necessarily for the wellbeing of the individual stock trader/investor.

B. Expert advice taken at face value without research can easily create more and bigger money-losing trades.

C. Following true leadership expertise can result in great advice, insights and training to produce money-making stock trades and avoid making money-losing stock trades.

Now that you have learned Mistake # 8, the Difference Between and Expert and EX PURT Advice, we can focus on Mistake # 9, Not Enough Time to Trade.

Mistake #9

"I'm Busy."

Mistake #9 is not enough time to trade, thinking this has to be a full-time job.

Why is it a mistake?

Most traders do not have enough time to research trades, place trades at the right time and follow up to execute a profitable trade or exit a money-losing trade.

What are the consequences of making this mistake and how critical are they? There are 2 parts: Time Commitment and Frustrations.

Time commitment

1. Traders think that in order to make successful trades, it has to be a full-time job with an 8 hour per day commitment. This is what happened to day traders too.
2. Without a written trading plan, traders don't create a step-by-step action plan which can be timed to know how long it takes you to find, research, enter and exit a trade.

3. Did not get into the trade and exit a trade at the right time because they didn't have the time to be a successful stock trader.

Frustrations

1. Traders place themselves at a distinct disadvantage when the decks of the trading world are already stacked against them.
2. Trading results are unpredictable.
3. Extreme frustration from making stupid trades, money-losing trades, hoping it comes back up to break even trades.

What should they do instead?

A. Have a written stock trading plan that has specific steps that can be timed. You know that it takes you, for example, 5 minutes to research a trade, so you can build a timeframe for trades.
B. Traders need to get their strategy in place, their trading tools in place, know how to time the stock market and know how much time it takes for them to place a successful trade.
C. Need to dedicate a set number of minutes and hours it takes daily to research, place and have entry and exits plan in place and set aside that time commitment.

Insight story

As I began as a full-time trader on May 1, 1999, I had bought a stock trading training plan for $3,000. I went to the first live audience training and got insights, tools and strategies to trade with.

I went home and set up my trading desk in my home office. I set up a wall-mounted TV and had everything set to go. I woke up at 6 a.m.—I'm on Pacific Standard Time—and I logged onto my computer and started checking the news, pre-market updates and watching CNBC and listening to the commentary.

The market shuts down at 1 p.m., so that was the end of my trading day. Later that evening I researched stocks, news and updates to the training center and subscriptions I had bought.

It was an exciting time because it was the dot-com boom and almost everything I traded made money. It was a trader's high and I was riding it. I made a small fortune, God it was fantastic.

After the dot-com boom ended on March 11 in 2000, I rode the dot-com bomb all the way down, not knowing what a down cycle meant. I made that fortune and then blew that fortune just as fast. I'd never experienced a bad down cycle before. Being an optimistic person in life, I felt the market was going to come back soon. I had that state of trading called hope, which is one of the worst traits to have as a trader.

After the meltdown known as the Internet bubble, I realized that I was a full-time trader putting in overtime with research. As I traded forward, I always looked for ways to shortcut the amount of time and money I spent as a trader.

During this timeframe I never had a written trading plan and it took me a long time to finally come up with one. As the years went by, I ended up making the written trading plan simple and effective for me to follow my trading rules.

What should you do if you have already made this mistake? How do you fix it? This a two-part action plan: Exit Trades and Research Your Time Spent Trading.

Exit trades

1. Finish up your open trades and shut them down per your rules of your trading plan or if you're seat-of-the-pants trading ASAP.
2. STOP TRADING!!!
3. Restart trading once you commit to having X amount of time to research, enter and exit trades.

Research your time spent trading

1. Time how long it takes to research your trade, place your trade, watch your trade and exit your trade. No judgment, just a report card on where your time is spent in trading in a whole weeks' time from Monday until Sunday, all seven days.
2. See what days you spend your time on? Are some days better than others? Are some times in the day or night better for researching?

3. Determine what time and times you can dedicate to your trading job, put that in writing and make a commitment to this plan.

How do we prevent making this mistake moving forward?

Because of the research in the previous section with the research action plan, you know what time you have to work with.

A. Write out a one-page trading schedule of times you use and have available to use in your trading profession.
B. Change your mindset that trading is a full-time job.
C. The idea in a job is trading time for money at a set rate. Have a new paradigm, a mind shift.

Here is how you can get results faster, easier, and more efficiently:

Three parts: Research, Time and Tools.

Research

1. Find a resource that gives you a way to time your stock trades.
2. Find a service that provides you a stock trading program that gives you stock selections to consider to trade on.
3. Research and learn to use entry and exits points with tools and trailing stops. Many

trading and brokerage companies have exiting tools and training for free.

Time

1.   Have a printed yearly calendar that gives you the framework to place your trades. Get mine from

     www.howtotradeinthestockmarket.com/cooltools/tradingcalendar – it's FREE.
2.   Dedicate a set amount of time each day for the functions for a trade, research, placing a trade, following a trade and exiting a trade.
3.   Use entry and exits points with tools and trailing stops as time-savers.

Tools

1.   Use Worden.com as your master trading tool because they give you a whole tool set, traders' commentary and a traders' forum at one of the most reasonable prices I have ever seen. They are the real deal: straightforward, focused on independent traders and started as a family business with three successful generations of traders' insights and wisdoms.
2.   Join a traders' coaching group and learn how to become a smarter and better trader from a teacher and fellow traders.
3.   Use a trading company for your stock trading account that has a mobile app. Use your smart

phone to track your trade from making it, to following it to adjusting your trailing stop based on your trade's performance.

The key

You are making so much an hour, if you are working at a job, being a manager, running your own business, retired on a fixed income. You make X an hour and that's your rate. Determine that and write it on a sticky note on your computer. The goal is to dramatically change that rate.

Your goal is to go to a 2X, 5X, 10 X or much dramatic rate on that same page of paper. Let say you're at $20 an hour and you go to 2X, which is $40 an hour. Every hour you spend in the trading process doubles your wages.

Why not invest more where you make the biggest bang. Mind shift!

40 hours per week averages to 2080 hours a week, which is $41,600 a year. Everything you invest in time to become a successful trader will grow you to go from the trading time for money formula to less time for more money if you treat this like a business. Make the time to become a successful trader.

Cool tool

Use the free written calendar and earnings season information to build your trading knowledge and platform on.

www.Howtotradeinthestockmarket.com/cooltool/master calendar

Summary

A. Set up a daily time to research, place, follow up on and exit a trade.

B. Don't get distracted by TV, advertising, or research that drains away valuable time to focus on your trade.

C. Automate any one of the pieces of trading to cut down on the time required to trade successfully. Today you can even use your smart phone for accessing your trading account and apps for your mobile trading tools.

Traders get trapped into thinking the way to be successful in the trading profession requires a vast amount of time and commitment equal to that of a full 40-hour job. Getting smart about the trading strategy, tools, training and cool tools will allow you to quickly bust this mindset and myth.

Now that Mistake #9, About Time, is shattered, we can move on how to avoid Mistake #10, Hanging on to Money-Losing Trades.

Mistake #10

"That's Just the Way It Is."

Mistake #10 is hanging on to a money-losing trade

Why is it a mistake?

Traders turn to HOPE as a trading tool, strategy and trading plan.

Traders should have been schooled in education, research, strategies and their written trading plan that the way to make money trading is to cut your losses quickly and let your winners run.

Stock trading is about creating losing trades and traders need to integrate that into their trading.

What are the consequences of making this mistake and how critical are they?

1. Traders get frozen in making the decision to exit a trade per their trading plans.
2. Traders lose even more money in their existing trade.
3. The trade goes to a zero value and you lose all your money.

Why and when do traders make these mistakes?
Two parts: Your Little Voice and Outside Advice

Your little voice,

1. It just can't go down anymore.
2. Well, I was already down so much money that I figured there was no point in getting out now.
3. I just have this feeling it's going to come back up again.

Outside advice

1. My broker said I should hold on to this one, it's coming back.
2. My friend/family member/coworker told me to buy this stock and even as it's going down I should hold it for the long run.
3. The mail flyer, e-mail or advisor newsletter said this is a winner and it will explode even after it pulls back.

Insight story

An emotional attachment to a stock that you are actively trading is one of the deadliest catch-22s you will face. Everyone wants to be a winner, have a winning (fill in the blank) life, wife, job, car, vacation and winning secret or advantage. The hot stock tip is one such item.

What you need to learn is that you are borrowing a stock ownership position and keeping it when it's doing what it's supposed to, which is making you money.

When the stock fails to meet your written trading plan, it's time to exit the trade. A great example comes to mind. You buy a car, you use it to take you where you want to go. When it start breaking down, you need to sell it or trade it for a more reliable car to take you where you want to go. Get the value out of the car and ditch it when it doesn't.

What should they do instead?

A. Have a written trading plan and follow it.
B. Have an exit strategy and use it on every trade.
C. Follow the money in Worden's proprietary trading platform and use it as your guide with a maximum amount you're willing to lose. If it's 10 percent, then it's a rule you have to follow.

What should you do if you have already made this mistake? How do you fix it?

1. Follow the money in the Worden proprietary trading platform and use it as your guide with a maximum amount you're willing to lose. If it's 10 percent, then it's a rule you have to follow.
2. If the Worden money stream pattern is going sideways, insert a tight stop per your trading plan.
3. If the Worden money stream is falling, make a decision to exit your trade. Cleaning out your money-losing trades is one of the hardest acts to do, but if you don't, you're stuck. Remember, a dollar is a dollar and any ones you can save let you live to trade another day.

How do we prevent making this mistake moving forward?

A. Follow the money in Worden's proprietary trading platform and use it as your guide with the maximum amount you are willing to lose.

B. As you place your next trade, place an exit or trailing stop order so there is a maximum you are willing to lose and no more.

C. Don't have loyalty feelings or commitments to a stock trade based on a broker, friend or family member. This is a business, so run it like one that profits.

Here is how you can get results faster, easier, and more efficiently:

1. Learn how to find good stocks to trade because they keep you in the trade.

2. Loyalty should be based on performance, and watch the money stream.

3. You will produce losing trades so cut them off early and move onto the next trade.

The key insight:

THE SOONER YOU LEARN TO GET RID OF LOSING TRADES QUICKLY AND DON'T LOOK BACK, THE QUICKER YOU'LL BECOME A SMARTER, SAVVY, SUCCESSFUL TRADER.

SAVVY, SUCCESFUL TRADERS ALSO DON'T MARRY THEIR STOCKS, THEY DATE THEM.

Now that we've learned to get past the mistake of holding onto money losing trades, we will move on to Mistake #11, Not Prepared Psychologically.

Mistake #11

"Hide from the Monster Under the Bed."

Mistake #11 is not being prepared for the psychological aspects of stock trading.

Why is it a mistake?

While there are a multitude of systems that teach successful trading, the reason the vast majority of traders lose money is because of the emotional reactions while trading.

The market is trying to tell you something but you are equally busy trying to impose your beliefs on the market (or your partner, life or your business).

"When you're unprepared, the market creeps up on you and makes you behave badly." —Dr. David Lake www.eftdownunder.com

What are the consequences of making this mistake and how critical are they? Two parts: Mindset and Beliefs

A. Mindset
1. You take trading personally, and have to win every trade.

2. Not wanting to close out a losing position.
3. Jumping in on a winning trade and taking the profit too quickly.

B. Beliefs

1. Thinking the market is out to get you.
2. Thinking the market has opinions, when only people do.
3. Makes you feel stupid and want to quit, only to complain the rest of your life how you were taken advantage of.

What should they do instead?

A. Don't take trading personally. It's a business; treat it as such.
B. Realize the market doesn't know you or care about you, good or bad.
C. Follow your written trading plan and/or trading platform guidelines with the lessons and training from this book. Cut your losses quickly and let your profits run.

Insight story

I have worked with many private clients in my coaching programs and will give Doug as an example. Doug was a very successful small business owner whose business was stable, made some money but was boring him. He got interested in stock trading from his brother-in-law, who was doing well trading.

Doug jumped in with his $5,000 initial investment with well-advertised TV ads Brokerage Company. He started out with some information from the trading company and bought a book, which he skimmed through in an evening. Heck, this was going to be easy, as he was a relatively successful business owner.

He began his trading and found that what he found in the business world to be normal thinking and actions didn't translate into winning stock trades. He didn't seem to place his trades at the right times because once he did place trades, they almost always started going down.

He started "feeling" that he was getting set up by the market the same way he felt when he went to Reno on his annual guys' trip. He expected to lose gambling, but he didn't in trading. His brother-in-law Larry called Doug and asked him how the trading was going.

Doug reluctantly started to tell him about how the market was out to get him and steal all his money. "Wall Street is no better than Reno or Las Vegas to me, they are all a bunch of thieves." Larry told him he had his doubts when he first started, but was fortunate to read the first book he bought cover to cover and start to get educated.

Larry was also a client of mine and he suggested Doug call me to get some additional training. I'm happy to report Doug was able to get past this victim mentality and see that he just had to work the trading business like he worked his own business, using the information in the beginning of this book with some coaching.

Doug got his trader mentality in line with being a successful stock trader. He has found peace of mind, feels more confident in his trading and has tamed the fear of failure.

What should you do if you have already made this mistake? How do you fix it? Two parts: Action and Reflect

A. Action

1. STOP TRADING IF YOU ARE UPSET.
2. STOP TRADING if you think and feel that you are taking trading too personally and the market is out to get you.
3. Make a decision based on your trading plan and close out your losing trades.

B. Reflect

1. Do stock autopsies to see where you went wrong in your trading rules or when you broke your rules.
2. Adjust and update your written trading plan.
3. Educate yourself: Read the book *Enjoy Emotional Freedom* by Dr. David Lake.

How do we prevent making this mistake moving forward?

You should not play the market, but work the market with your written plan and any systems or platforms you use. Trading is the activity of speculating in the market in order to gain an advantage financially. Think of this as your own business, regardless if its a little lemonade stand or any size of growing business.

Treat it as a business owner does.

Here is how you can get results faster, easier, and more efficiently:

The key:

Remember Mistakes #1 and #2 from the beginning of the book: Earnings calendars, earnings seasons, earnings release date and time and other significant events. Learn them and integrate them into your trading system.

Don't go it alone; get involved with a strong ongoing education program. How to time your trade is everything in setting up a winning trade.

Summary

1. Don't take trading and losing money personally.
2. STOP TRADING when you're stringing together too many losing trades; regroup with guidance from what you have learned or rules of your written trading plan and/or system.
3. Reread this book from the beginning, and integrate the lessons and tools that have been provided.

Now that we have prepared for the psychological aspects of trading, we will move on to the last mistake, #12, Impatience of Trading Correctly.

Mistake #12

"The 800-Pound Gorilla."

Mistake #12 is being impatient on trading correctly.

This mistake is not knowing about the Traders' Gold Dollar Coin: on one side is the Fear of Failure and on the other side, the Fear of Success. Once the trader starts making trades, they will be flipping the coin in every trade they make.

Why is it a mistake?

Traders worry about losing money and making money on every trade they make, most on a daily and even hourly to minute-by-minute timeframe. Poor traders worry about money in their trading account and not having enough. Rich traders worry about keeping what they have amassed and making more.

Because stock trading is a major life event and challenge in most people's lives, at some point their worst fears will be faced. Most stock traders choose to engage in trading in order to make money.

Most want to make enough to change their lives, whether it's additional income, replacement of present job income, retirement income or ultimate financial freedom.

By creating too many losing trades, the trader faces the fear that they have lost the money in their trading account and are failures.

By creating too many winning trades, the traders that create great amounts of wealth in sometimes short amounts of time will face the success and fear of making and having too much money.

Laugh as you may, but too many people have failures in their pasts that haunt them and as in the case of huge lottery winners, almost 90 percent lose their winnings within a 5-year timeframe.

What are the consequences of making this mistake and how critical are they?

1. Not knowing that you will hold this Traders' Gold Dollar Coin will cause you many sleepless nights, frustrations and second-guessing.
2. You will not be at peace with yourself; the chaos will cloud your judgment and ultimately freeze your ability to execute trades.
3. The trader will become one of the industry's estimated 95 percent failures that wash out.

Why and when do traders make this mistake?

A. When traders don't cut their trading losses quickly and don't let their profits run.
B. When they don't prepare themselves for the roller coaster ride of losing 5 out of 10 trades or worse.

C. When traders don't have a written trading plan and execute on it, rather trade by the seat of their pants.

What should they do instead?

1. Have a written trading plan that has rules for researching stock trades.
2. Have a written trading plan that enters trades that meet criteria and avoids trades that do not meet successful trading criteria.
3. Once the trade is made, cut your losses quickly and let your profitable trades run with a written exit strategy.

What should you do if you have already made this mistake? How do you fix it?

A. Review your open trades and consider exiting your trades per a written plan.
B. STOP TRADING.
C. Build a written trading plan that you can follow to guide you in your trading.

How do we prevent making this mistake moving forward?

1. Build or buy a solid written trading plan and implement it.
2. Realize that you will have losing trades and be prepared for them; all traders, even the most seasoned traders and trading companies, have many losing trades.

3. Be at peace and have time to research, review, place and exit a trade per your trading plan.

Here is how you can get results faster, easier, and more efficiently:

A. You have to invest both time and money into getting a very basic trading education.
B. You have to treat this like it is your own business, which means building a certain amount of time every day to research, place and follow a trade. This can be as little as 5 minutes a day.
C. Have an open trade checklist.

The key is, if you decided to earn a little more money every month, you could work overtime, find part-time job or start a business.

Each requires time and money. Why not invest in the tools and training to get you the biggest buck return in your trading success? In this book I have a list of cool tools, services and courses you can take to dramatically change the odds of placing successful trades in your favor.

Let's summarize the big picture:

1. Traders create losing trades because it's the nature of trading.
2. Losing trades create the fear of failure in traders.
3. Too many money-making trades cause traders to face the fear of success.
4. The way to control those fears is to have a written stock trading plan and trade accordingly.

5. When in doubt about your trading fears, stop trading.

That's the Top 12 Stock Trading Mistakes that Traders Make – time to move to the conclusion in this book.

Putting the Pieces Together

Now that you understand the Top 12 Mistakes Stock Traders Make that cost them time, money and frustrating sleepless nights – and how to fix them – let me share with you my checklist to make sure you avoid these mistakes like the plague.

Checklist

Here is the checklist, which contains specific questions to ask to make sure that you avoid these mistakes. All you have to do is just ask these questions and know your bases are covered. If you can answer "YES" to each question, you are good to go trading. If not, then make the adjustments needed to be successful.

1. Do I have a simple written trading plan that I follow in every trade? If not, make, get and use a basic plan. If nothing else, write out the steps you are already doing.

2. Do I have a compelling reason to trade this stock? There has to be a reason for the stock to go up – have I identified it? This can be anything from a recommendation from friend to a professional pick.

3. Have I pulled out my printed trading calendar and identified where I am at with the specific timeframe I'm about to trade? If not, do this now.

4. Have I identified and written down the exact date and time for the company's next earnings release before placing the trade? If not, do this critical research step.

5. Have I pulled up my visual chart of candlesticks, money flow and volume?

6. Have I double-checked money flow in the last 30 days to see the positive pattern I'm looking for? If not, you need to buy this Worden.com service; it's the one service that will change the odds in your favor.

7. Do I have peace of mind, clear focus and time for making a successful trade? If I'm distracted with a huge project, stressed relationship and/or going on vacation, I stop trading because a stressed mind is a huge reason for making money-losing trades.

8. Have I decided on what maximum loss I'm willing to take before exiting a trade? If not, decide now on a number – 10, 20, 30 percent – and write it out. I'm placing a $1,000 trade and I'm willing to lose $200, max.

9. Have I set a trailing stop based on maximum loss I'm willing to make? If not, set up the trade because

hanging onto losing trades is the quickest way to busting your trading account.

10. Have I set a goal to how much I want to make in this trade? If not, write it down in your written trading plan.

11. Have I set a trailing stop to let my winning trades keep going until they fail for me to capture the full upside of my trade? The second biggest reason traders are not successful is they don't let their winners run.

12. I decide by my written trading plan and checklist to place the trade. If not, you need to check off your preflight checklist like any commercial pilot would because if you don't, you're flying by the seat of your pants.

13. At least once a day I monitor my trade via my smart phone mobile app. Following your trade lets you know how the trade trailing stops are performing.

14. I have a trade review after the market closes to review my trade and adjust it to my written trading plan and review of money flow in the trade. If you don't follow the money, you will be at a disadvantage.

15. Have I closed out my trade by writing down my results, successful or unsuccessful, and kept score? If

not, do this step now. When you write down the trade and results, it's easier to do a stock trade autopsy in a training I provide that sharpens your trading success.

Final Thoughts

I specifically chose researching your next trade's earnings release date and time as my #1 Mistake.

Regardless whether you're a beginner, intermediate or advanced trader, this one piece of information will change the ratio of placing winning or losing trades in your favor.

Even some of my most successful advanced coaching clients, friends and business colleagues say this insight and trading tool has made them a better, more successful trader.

The traders that I have met that use automated systems to trade as a platform have told me that once they research the trade and plug that event into their review report, that date many times triggers their exit from a trade.

They capture the profit and avoid losing the gain.

The next step I would suggest is to build a SIMPLE written trading plan and plug in the checklist to build out your written trading plan. You can pick and choose from the list above and build out your trading plan.

Use the resource that is provided in this book to start the process.

If you have a written trading plan, then pick any of the checklist steps or tools you don't have and incorporate them. You will amaze yourself with the results you achieve in future trades.

"PLAN YOUR TRADE and TRADE YOUR PLAN" is what a wonderful mentor, Mike, taught me for ultimate success. He also shared what I believe now: "Your success is my business and reward for mentoring and coaching you." Thanks, Coach Mike.

I hope you enjoyed this book and that it enriches your life and the lives of your family, friends and community. It is a privilege to share this information with you and I wish you trading success and ultimate financial freedom.

I have a favor to ask. If you enjoyed this book and benefited from the insights, wisdom and trading tools, **would you please take the time to favorably rate this book on Amazon**? You can help me achieve my goal of helping the independent trader be more successful against the big trading companies on Wall Street.

Thank you in advance,

Pete

Next Steps

Your next steps are actually pretty straightforward and simple.

Avoid these mistakes like the plague.

Again, all it takes is one mistake to create more losing stock trades.

I said right from the beginning that I have made all these mistakes and lost a million-plus dollars.

Take the path to change the odds in your favor and creating money-making stock trades without the costly education process.

Use the checklist to create more winning stock trades and avoid more money-losing stock trades. Shift the balance of power and odds of making more money by making stock trades to your side of trading.

Next time you are going to fly on a commercial flight (hopefully from your profitable trading for a vacation), would you want to have your pilot use a preflight checklist or fly by the seat of his or her pants?

Please, PLAN YOUR TRADE and TRADE YOUR PLAN.

Don't Be Left Behind

Your **Personal Invitation from Peter Schneider**

Because you bought my book I'd like **personally INVITE YOU** to visit my blog and subscribe for updates so you can get the latest key insights into what's working in the world of stock trading, cool tools and new programs.

If you want to learn to make more money-making trades and avoid making money-losing trades, then here's what I'd like to invite you to do.

Go ahead and log on to www.howtotradeinthesockmarket.com and sign up for a free account. It takes less than 30 seconds and could very well revolutionize the way you think, take action and produce more stock winning trades.

That means you'll be able to get all the latest developments in stock trading, ALERTS, the reminders to pay attention to earning calendars, coming earnings seasons and key upcoming critical market events.

You will also get alerts to my forthcoming book "HOW TO TIME YOUR TRADE – for Greater Profits." As a special treat, you will receive my first chapter in advance of the book's release in the middle of 2014.

Again, signing up is easy and FREE. Point your web browser to www.howtotradeinthestockmarket.com and sign up for a free account (we promise to never spam or share your account information and name with anyone).

So if you have enjoyed this book and want to take your stock trading to the next level, head on over to www.howtotradeinthestockmarket.com right now and get on board for free.

What do you have to lose but your hard-earned money?